God's Promises

for

the Family Circle

God's Promises *for* the Family Circle

A Collection of Inspirational Poetry

MARIONETTE SIMMONS

Order this book online at www.trafford.com
or email orders@trafford.com

Most Trafford titles are also available at major online book retailers.

Scripture quotations marked KJV are from the Holy Bible, King James Version
(Authorized Version). First published in 1611. Quoted from the KJV Classic
Reference Bible, Copyright © 1983 by The Zondervan Corporation.

Scripture quotations marked NIV are taken from the *Holy Bible, New
International Version*®. *NIV*®. Copyright © 1973, 1978, 1984 by International
Bible Society. Used by permission of Zondervan. All rights reserved.

Scripture quotations marked AMP are from *The Amplified Bible*, Old Testament copyright ©
1965, 1987 by the Zondervan Corporation. *The Amplified Bible*, New Testament copyright ©
1954, 1958, 1987 by The Lockman Foundation. Used by permission. All rights reserved.

Print information available on the last page.

ISBN: 978-1-4907-6483-2 (sc)
ISBN: 978-1-4907-6484-9 (hc)
ISBN: 978-1-4907-6485-6 (e)

Library of Congress Control Number: 2015914308

Trafford rev. 09/02/2015

 www.trafford.com

North America & international
toll-free: 1 888 232 4444 (USA & Canada)
fax: 812 355 4082

Dedication

To my Lord and Savior
I give thanks to the Father for the inspiration and for giving me the fortitude to stick with it and go ahead and glorify Him with my time and my God-given talent and for breathing His Word into me and bringing forth life through words, which I now share with others.
I dedicate this to my church family, the Open Door Christian Assembly, for their prayers and support. And special thanks to Pastor George Smith who encouraged me to press on and as he says, "I can't wait to see the finished work."

To my nephew Earl
Earl, thanks for always listening and saying, "Aunt Mary, let God continue to use you. Your words are always a source of encouragement to me and right on time. Let God continue to have his way."

To my mom, Eloise Tuzo
Thanks for being there to listen and be my sounding board when I needed to bounce ideas off on you, and for listening when I wanted to read one of my poems to you to receive your invaluable feedback and wisdom. There is no one like you and I give thanks to you. To show my appreciation, I dedicate the poem "What does the word Mother mean to me" to you.

Introduction

As I step back and reflect on my life and the accomplishments, responses, sales, and accolades received from my first book published in 2007, Life's Challenges, Experiences and Blessings, I can say that it is by God's grace and mercy that I was inspired to move on to book number two, which you have the pleasure of reading and holding in your hand, God's Promises for the Family Circle. Many of my friends and loyal readers have encouraged me to move on and just do it. I continue to love writing, but more than that, I love to encourage others by my words, and I pray that something that I say would motivate them and give them a sense of hope, as I share my biblical-based poetry as indicated by this book's title, God's Promises for the Family Circle. You'll never know whose life you may touch or change with your words, which we have been taught as we strive to be an evangelist in this dark world, to shed the light of God in what we say and do. I strive to live out my church's creed, "We are ministers and our lives are a ministry." I pray that someone may be persuaded by this book and find salvation.

I can say that each time I put pen to paper, it is the work of the Lord showing forth; and I pray that someone who picks up this book and reads through the pages will be encouraged, inspired, and uplifted by what he reads or will have fun in the word search section as he basks in the second section: "Prayer Time and Bible Word Search.". "Faith without works is dead" as we are told in James 2:20b (KJV), so I step out by faith and release this book forward. I have always said and tried to live by this maxim, we are blessed to be a blessing. My Pastor, Dean Smith, would often say, "Don't sit on the gifts and talents that God has given to you," so here I again share these gifts and talents. As I endeavor to live out this creed each day, I pray that my ministry here will go forth far and wide and encourage someone to minister by faith to someone else that he encounters. "For I am not ashamed of the gospel of Christ: for it is the power of God unto salvation to every one that believeth," Romans 1:16a (KJV).

May you find time in your life as you read my words and see that God can bring you out of whatever you are going through in life. Enjoy some of the lighthearted poems I have shared over the years with family and friends displayed in the first section of this book. It speaks to all the remarks entitled, "Encouragement" and Lord knows I have had much.

I thank God as he continues to inspire me. He is my main focus, and I have been blessed to write poetry as well as to write music through my poetry. I am also blessed with the ability to sing. The two talents have now gone hand in hand and is now opening another door of blessings. I am thankful for those in my church fellowship at the Open Door Christian Assembly, for their encouragement and prayers as I will soon realize both of my dreams, the writing and publishing of this collection of poems and soon to be released my first gospel CD entitled, God's Promises to be released sometime in 2015.

As you browse through the various sections of this book, my prayer is that you will laugh, have fun, be convicted to be challenged and changed, but most of all, to be drawn nearer to God. Find him if you don't know him and invite him into your heart.

If you can find yourself or words that speak to you in Part three, "Family Circle," take heart, it is easy reading for the whole family, of any age. Read it to your children or let them enjoy it for themselves.

When you want to relax in some quiet time with God, go straight to section four, "Lord, Speak to Me.". I am sure there is something for

everyone found somewhere in this book, so read on, relax, bask in the presence of God and be blessed.
I believe in making the most of the gifts God gives on loan to us during our lifetime; therefore, I share one of mine with you.

May God's many blessings be upon the readers of this book!

Contents

Prayer of Thanks

Lord, I'm thankful that you have blessed me with this talent to write about you and to share words of encouragement with others about you and your Word.

My prayer is to share this book with many, especially those that are searching for something more than their everyday existence. For those who feel lost or trapped and are looking for a way out, my prayer is that he or she finds the Lord Jesus, the Christ, for He is the Way the Truth and the Life and apart from Him there is no other.

My hope is that something that I have written or have read in this book will draw them to you, and be able to experience it for themselves, so that they too can know the joy, peace, and laughter that you bring to my life every day.

Let some kind word written help them in life to heed or even serve as a gentle rebuke to help them find their way. So teach us to number our days, that we may apply our hearts unto wisdom (Psalm 90:12 - KJV).

I'm thankful for the gifts that God has laid before me. I offer them back to Him in thanksgiving and praise. I count it a privilege that I can share with others my talents, time, and God's promises for my life.

I am thankful first and foremost to God, and I am also thankful to those who have stood by me and supported my every endeavor; to them I owe a hearty thank you.

Lest we forget, all things come from thee, O Lord and therefore I acknowledge, praise, and give thanks unto you.

Amen.

The author, Marionette Simmons.

Part One

"Encouragement"

-I-
-Trust in-
-BELIEVE in-
-And rely upon the Master of-
-ENCOURAGEMENT-

GOD the FATHER
JESUS the SON-
-And the HOLY SPIRIT.-

The Trinity

"I Am God's Voice on the Earth"

We often say these words as believers,
"If you can use anything, Lord, you can use me."

But are we open to be used or are we lip-syncing through this journey?

When we are called to pray or should be praying and interceding in our closets, are we too occupied with our own stuff to be bothered?

I'm speaking to myself here, as often said, "I am the first partaker of this one!"

As I strive to be God's voice on this Earth
I will try to get myself together first
But in this flesh I fail, so I will look until the hills from whence cometh my help for I know it comes from the Lord.

I need to ask God to awaken the parts in me that are asleep
I will ask God to burst forth for I have been saved to serve and not to be still

I will ask God to shed away the dead parts of my life, so he can shine like the morning light
I will ask him to speak to me, so he can speak through me, so I hear his voice and not my own.

I will be the first partaker so that I can speak out of my experience
He has brought me through the test of time, not a textbook or hearsay
I will ask the Holy Spirit to be my guide, so I can get understanding and impart God's Word with wisdom

I will ask him to fill me with his word, so that when I don't have it before me, it is already in me.

Then, I will see that God turns my darkness into morning
My fears into peace
My dry places into flourishing hills
My valleys into mountain tops
My sadness into gladness
He gives me beauty for ashes

I can take all of these many blessings and share what I know and have lived and tell someone along the way
Tell someone that God loves them, cares for them, and is intimately acquainted with all their ways
Even to the point where He has numbered every hair on their head
I can be God's voice on the Earth.

Reflecting on God's Goodness

Step back and take a look at your past
Tell me when you look back there, was it a blast
Or was it filled with a void leading to destruction and pain
Before the Father came into your life and cancelled your guilty stain?

Many of us say, "Oh I was not that bad"
This is the trick of the enemy to keep you unfulfilled and sad
He dangles many carrots of flashy things before your very eyes
To take you away from God's promises, to take you far from his prize

But when you experience the goodness of the Lord
You soon forget those empty times that kept you tied in cords
Don't be fooled by the subtle things that try to lure you back
Every day seek God's face, read His Word it will keep you on track

Surrender is the key, although it may seem hard at times
But when you experience the goodness of God, real treasures you will find
So shout and praise, raise your hands, and celebrate each and every day
Reflecting on God's goodness, renew your spirit and pray

For He will never leave you nor forsake you at anytime
These are not empty words, but encouragement for your soul and mind
Live my brother, live my sister, be encouraged on your walk
Reflect on the goodness of God in your conduct and your talk.

For truly God's worthy and your hope in him secure

He'll carry all your burdens and keep your life's path straight and sure
These are just a few things that we can reflect upon
Remember saints, with the Lord the battle's already won

We are more than conquerors; we're the head and not the tail
Believe it, receive it, don't let it be a cliché, let it prevail
When I reflect on God, the Father, this is what happens to me
I live in hope, I live in joy, and I live worry-free

He said to me: Do not give thought for tomorrow
Because he dresses the lilies and even feeds the sparrow
He said that he will give me what I stand in need of, he owns all the hills
The cattle all belong to him, so surrender and follow his will

Read his word every day to prepare yourself for the journey ahead
Pray, meditate, and intercede, put your burdens to bed
For he said his yoke is easy and his burden is light, so don't keep them on your head
Leave them at the altar and walk away in victory instead

Trust him where you can't trace him and exercise your faith
This is how I choose to live, giving thanks for his mercy and his grace
So next time you stop and think things are not going your way
Reflect on God's goodness and a new outcome you will display

For darkness and light cannot co-exist, darkness has to go out of sight
And when God's goodness shows forth, the devil is put to flight
Don't let the enemies' distractions be your downfall
Call on the Savior, He will surely answer your call.
Now step back and reflect on God's goodness.

A Mother's Heart

Luke 6:45b - AMP says, ". . . for out of the abundance (overflow) of the heart his mouth speaks."

When a woman carries a child, many hormones rage and many emotions flood her heart in abundance
For those who do not get to experience childbirth but have a passion for children, they too experience much emotions of the heart.
Mothers, as God has spoken life into your existence, we also have a responsibility to speak life into our children.

A mother's heart is full of love at the sight of her little girl or boy
A mother's heart is proud when her child says her name for the first time and she is elated with joy
A mother's heart is made glad by every accomplishment of her child
A mother's heart is saddened when her child disappoints mankind, but only for a while
A mother's heart grieves when her child experiences death during her life span
A mother's heart rejoices when her child follows in the path of righteousness and seeks God's hand
A mother's heart bleeds when her child is in turmoil or pain
A mother's heart knows no bounds for the love of her child is never in vain
A mother's heart allows her to love those who she bore and others she may encounter
A mother wears her heart on her sleeve, not because she chooses to, but because she is a mother.

A mother cares
A mother shares

A mother laughs
A mother cries
A mother is dependable

Mothers have been portrayed as all wise to many a child over the years
Let the wisdom of God guide you, mothers, into all truth and understanding
So that out of the abundance of your heart, the mouth will speak to your children.

Dispelling the Negative and Accentuating the Positive: A-Z

A - *Instead of showing and portraying **A**nger all the time*
*Let's replace it with **Anticipation** of something good happening*

B - *Instead of **B**ashing and **B**elittling people*
*Let's **Build** them up*

C - *Instead of **C**asting down and **C**utting off someone*
*Let us learn to **Compliment** them*

D - *Instead of **D**estruction and **D**egrading the moral fiber of any man*
*Let us seek **Dependence** on and **Deliverance** from the Father*

E - *Let us not be **E**nvious and **E**gotistical in our ways*
*But instead be **Extroverted** and **Examples** of what's good and not bad*

F - *Instead of **F**ussing and **F**ighting at every turn on every issue*
*Let's have **Faith** in God and find **Favor** with your fellow man*

G - *Help to dispel the **G**angs and the **G**uns in this world*
*And replace it with **Goodwill** and **Gratitude***

H - *Instead of **H**arassing your brother and sister and being **H**ot-headed*
*Find ways to bring **Harmony** and instill **Hope***

I - *Many times we are **I**ndifferent and **I**mprisoned in our minds, homes, and in our jobs*
*So get **Involved** and take an **Interest** in the things that surround you each day*

J - Let us not be Judgmental of others and Jealous of their accomplishments
For <u>Judgment</u> belongs to God so let the <u>Joy</u> of the Lord be our strength

K – Let us not Kill the hope of a man by squashing his dreams
But instead show <u>Kindness</u> and <u>Kindle</u> his aspirations

L - Let us not partake of Lewd conversations or Label a man by his outer appearance
Counter that with <u>Lasting</u> words of wisdom and <u>Love</u> for all mankind

M – Do not Monopolize situations or Malign the character of anyone
Instead <u>Motivate</u> positive thinking and let the <u>Manifestation</u> of it show forth

N – Neglecting responsibilities and promoting Negative behavior is unwise counsel
Therefore, let your actions be <u>Noble</u> and your words <u>Noteworthy</u>

O – Oppression is the stamp of cowardice and Obsession borders on idolatry
So let the <u>Omnipresent</u> and <u>Omniscient</u> God take hold of you and lead you to <u>Obedience</u>

P – Don't get caught up in Pornography or the Peer Pressure of life
Let <u>Purity</u> prevail and accept yourself for the person that you are

Q – Spouses and friends, do not Quarrel at every opportunity
Instead bring <u>Quality</u> to your relationships by giving of your time and meaningful conversation.

R – *Riotous* and *Reckless living cause you to have a *Restless* soul
But God has given us <u>Restoration</u> for our souls, <u>Revival</u> in our
hearts, and an everlasting <u>Relationship</u> with him, take advantage of
the blessings bestowed upon you.*

S – *Sickness* and *Starvation has plagued many a nation
So give <u>Selflessly</u> and let the <u>Salvation</u> of the Lord guide you to help
make a difference*

T – *Tyranny* and *Toughness has its place in the battlefield, let's not
take it out of context
<u>Tenderness</u> also has its place and must be administered with the right
<u>Touch</u> and at the right <u>Time</u>*

U – *You can be **U**nloved, **U**nacceptable by society, and **U**nsafe,
which seemingly puts you in a very bad light
But the **<u>U</u>ncompromising** love of Christ can make you <u>**U**pright</u> in
spirit and <u>**U**plift</u> you where society has no bounds.*

V – *Vandalism* and *Vindictive behavior are outburst and outcries for
help
Let's be <u>Visionaries</u>, with <u>Vested</u> interest in cultivating a productive
nation and enhance the life of someone to stop the cycle.*

W – *Waste can pertain to garbage or one's life, let's heed the
Warning signs
Be a <u>**W**itness</u> of the gospel while you have the chance, and <u>**W**eather</u>
the storms with prayers while you have time.*

X – *Xenophobic (intolerant and racist) people are shallow and are
normally not comfortable in their own skin
But learn to be <u>**X**enodochial</u> (friendly to a stranger), for you never
know when you are entertaining angels.*

Y – Yelling at someone quite often doesn't accomplish anything
Yet if you <u>Yearn</u> to get your point across, a calm still voice may <u>Yield</u>
the desired result.

Z – Zymotic (fermentation of a disease) of malaria could wipe out a
nation
So let's be <u>Zealous</u> in our efforts to stamp out the disease by taking
precautionary measures and always accentuate the positive and
dispel the negative.

Jesus, Crucifixion, Burial, and Resurrection

For God so loved the world, that he gave his only begotten Son, that whosoever believeth in him should not perish, but have everlasting life. John 3:16 - KJV

CRUCIFIXION
C   Christ suffered and died for our sins at Calvary
R   Rest in the Lord all ye his people for He has set us free
U   Understand the magnitude of the ultimate sacrifice
C   Compassion is ours because He gave His Life
I   Innocent blood was shed for the redemption of our souls
F   Forget not all His benefits toward us, for in the Bible we are told
I   I am the Lord your God, your hope, your help, your peace
X   X-rays by the Lord examine our heart and help to guide our feet
I   Invite Him into your heart today, afresh and anew
O   Open up yourself in obedience and His will you shall do
N   New mercy is yours today because the Lord has seen you through.

BURIAL
B   Be still and know that I am God
U   Untie the bounds of the enemy and show the power of the Lord
R   Revival is also yours; Jesus took away the keys to hell
I   Invitation given, rejection and refusal, O what stories to tell
A   Affliction and evangelism has gone forth, encouragement and the like
L   Love poured out on your behalf, calamity and strife.

RESURRECTION

R Relationship with the Father, Son, and Holy Spirit is yours because He rose again

E Ever making intercession for His people, no more stripes and no more pain

S Salvation is presented to you; He wants you to invite Him in

U Unbelief has no place; He shed His blood for that too and for all of our sins

R Risen Savior, forgive your people for they know not what they do

R Repent and return to God, O ye people, Let Him fulfill His purpose in you

E Edify and encourage your brethren and exhort the people by God's Word

C Consecrate yourself you set aside people, for the gospel to be heard

T Test and trials you will endure, but I've sent the Comforter

I Intercession I make for you each day, for my children here on earth

O Obedience is what I ask of you, my blessings will abound

N Never look to the left or the right for I hold you in my palm.

In John 14:6 - KJV, Jesus said, I am the way the truth and the life, no man cometh unto the Father but by me.

Believer, receive the CRUCIFIXION, BURIAL, and RESSURECTION in your bosom today, recognize the full impact of what Jesus did at Calvary for you and live in the Power, Might, Authority, Blessings, Revelation, Hope, and all of God's riches that have been bestowed upon you.

Lord, What Must I Sacrifice?

Many people don't know what it is to sacrifice
What is sacrifice?
Sacrifice is something you give up to obtain something you want or
that is far better than what you have.

Lord, show me what I need to sacrifice
To bring me closer to you and be more pleasing in your sight
Help me to let go of this grip of things that holds me down
Let me not have you pry them from me, but learn to release them
and not be bound

Let me see that you will supply my every need
Reassure me that you have watered everything I sowed into seed
As you have poured out blessing toward me I can truly say
My life has changed for the better since you came my way

It is said in Your Word, (1 Samuel 15:22b - KJV) that "to obey is
better than sacrifice"
So help us to learn this lesson early to be at peace and not in strife
And as we go along life's journey and way
We can be glad your spirit drew us and we invited you in to stay.

Thank you for being my Savior and Lord.

A Woman of Wisdom

I found it quite amusing, the common things we share
Since I know you're a woman of wisdom with your words of care
I have been listening attentively as your sentiments were displayed
As cards were read, written by you, I stood in awe and was amazed.

Wisdom of the old passed on to the youth is a precious gift to give
For as children of God we are taught to share and encourage as we live
You never know whose life you are touching from day to day
Or who you may be encouraging as you go on your merry way

It's like the way you light up the room when your favorite song is sung
"Come let's stroll down blessed boulevard," for you know the
battle's won

The psalmist says in (Psalm 92:1- KJV):
It is a good thing to give thanks unto the Lord and to sing praises
unto thy name O most High
For we know that each day as we are given life, we have something to
thank God for inside.

My prayer for you is to keep on pressing on the upward way
That God will strengthen you each and every day
That his hand will be upon you in your sitting and lying down
And you will always wear a smile and never draw a frown

For as long as we have the Lord on our side we have hope to carry on
and take each day in stride.

Be encouraged, my sister and friend.
Hold on every day to God's unchanging hand.

A New Mother's Perspective

I've written many tributes to mothers before
Now I have a new perspective as a mother, I've opened a new door
Motherhood is not just something that arrives one day
They're qualities that are awakened in you, waiting to be displayed.

I speak today as a new mother with a different point of view
Loving each moment as I watch my daughter grow and learn something new.

When you hold that life in your hands for the very first time
And sit and remember when your mother sang you nursery rhymes
You know that God has blessed you and you've come to a new stage in your life
It's not just you to look after anymore but also this precious life

A mother's love cannot be compared
A mother's love is always shared
A mother's hand reaching out displays to her child her love
It should also be the hand of discipline as the "Word" is given from above

Motherhood is a challenge that we face with each passing day
As we give God thanks for these gems to nurture and encourage them not to stray
Motherhood is exciting and drastically changes the very core of your life
With the support of family and friends, it's truly worth the fight.

A mother is like a ring
A never ending circle of love

MARIONETTE SIMMONS

Her children are like the jewels and gems that fit inside
She molds them to fit just right
And takes care of them as they stay ever so close
One day the gem may fall away
But she always keeps a close eye, to put them back where they belong.

Mothers I salute you today for being the women you are.

A Tribute to a Friend, Colleague, and a Sister in Christ

We've worked together for many years
Toiled through the hard work, also enjoyed the laughter and the tears
Remembering the times we've shared both on and off the job
And being able to share with her, "her trust in the Lord."

Many times we don't get to express how we really feel
And time passes us by and it's left unrevealed
As fellow colleagues and also as friends
We send to you heartfelt sympathies and God's comforting hand.

From the department she has left behind
We'll miss you, we love you, and you'll always be in our hearts and minds
And from this company (AIG) which she served so aptly
We say thank you, for allowing us a part of her life, and may God be with you and your family.

I remember telling Gilbert one day
God is going to finish just what he started
She began with him and "Praise God" she has gone home to glory
And we can be assured that she has fought the good fight of faith
And I admire her for her fighting spirit.

For those of us who do not understand
Eternal life is God's perfect plan
She died one death a long time ago
God ordained this eternity and it is so.

MARIONETTE SIMMONS

To the family I say, hold on to God's unchanging hand
And in Christ the solid rock you stand
He heals the broken-hearted,
And he is a comforter and a friend.

Isaiah 11:6b – KJV "… And a little child will lead them."

Part Two

"Prayer Time and Bible Word Search"

Prayer for Families

Father, you called families into existence from the beginning of time when you formed Adam out of the dust of the earth and breathed into him and he became a living soul and then formed Eve from his rib and together they became one (bone of my bone and flesh of my flesh) and told them to be fruitful and multiply and fill the earth.

This was evident that you ordained families by your words and actions. And in your word whenever you speak of blessings, you often say from generations to generations, therefore showing us that your thoughts are far beyond our thoughts and your way worth seeking out and you do not just look at what we see as the family in front of us but the generations to come.

Father, you have also given us instructions to follow regarding marriage, rearing our children, life, and godliness. I pray that we, as your children, follow the mandate set before us, that we cover our families, our household with your love and wisdom. You set the example of this in your word and through your Son, Jesus Christ. May we continue to intercede for our loved ones and bring them often before you. In Jesus's name, we pray. Amen.

Eight Letter Words in the Bible

A	L	M	T	N	E	P	S	S	H	T
Y	O	I	E	D	R	E	A	B	B	A
T	H	G	O	A	P	C	C	S	E	H
M	A	R	M	Y	S	E	H	U	R	C
C	H	I	R	B	A	Z	L	A	O	G
V	C	A	O	I	V	L	A	H	D	L
N	A	Z	N	I	S	A	E	C	I	P
H	C	A	U	P	H	O	A	R	M	B
T	E	R	P	D	E	F	A	M	E	E
M	Y	O	D	E	L	S	P	I	M	R
S	I	M	I	S	M	E	I	L	E	R
E	A	I	T	B	S	C	H	I	L	N
H	N	A	P	A	B	O	R	G	I	O
P	E	G	Y	S	H	O	N	O	R	A
I	A	N	G	H	G	I	E	N	G	R
T	A	L	A	U	G	V	R	E	T	Y
E	P	A	S	K	U	I	T	S	H	E
S	W	P	U	T	S	A	P	D	C	P
A	R	H	A	P	E	G	O	R	E	H
N	I	C	H	I	L	T	S	W	O	R
I	T	N	E	R	D	U	P	I	H	S

Almighty	*Ephesian*	*Promised*	*Worships*
Apostles	*Families*	*Punished*	*Zach aria*
Augustus	*Galatian*	*Religion*	
Baptisms	*Laodicea*	*Remember*	
Children	*My Savior*	*Repented*	
Churches	*Nazareth*	*Sabbaths*	
Egyptian	*Neighbor*	*Shepherd*	
Epaphras	*Preaches*	*Strength*	

Prayer of Confession and Faith

Dear Lord, I will lift up mine eyes unto the hills from whence cometh my help, for it comes from the Lord who made heaven and earth. Thank you, kind Father, for allowing us to see another day. Thank you for your peace that surpasses all understanding. Thank you for being our shelter in the time of storm. Thank you for being our way maker and our burden bearer. Thank you for being Jehovah Shalom, our peace. Thank you for being Jehovah Jireh, our provider. We have come into your presence with thanksgiving and to magnify your name and to worship you, dear Lord. We have not come to church but we recognize that we are the church on the earth that you, Lord, called and commissioned us before your ascension from this earth to go forth and make disciples and to feed the flock and increase the kingdom.

Help us, dear Lord, to forsake this flesh each day and take up our cross and follow you. Help us to die daily to self and say not my will but thy will be done on earth as it is in heaven. Breathe over us and fill us with your Holy Spirit afresh and anew. This is a new day that we have never seen before. We endeavor to be steadfast in our hearts to walk in holiness and in righteousness that is in right standing with you, Lord, and to help someone along the way of our day's journey, whether it be with a smile, a kind word or deed, that will show the love of God and also show who we are, your seed in the earth, your children.

The world is looking for something different than what it experiences daily. It is looking to the people of God to show and exhibit that there is more to this life than the mere destruction and hopelessness and sadness that many face day after day. Dear Lord, help us to stay in tune with you and be the rock on someone's shaky ground, to *share with him that it is not us who is the rock but Jesus Christ—the solid rock, the sure foundation, the lifter of our head, our refuge and strength on which we stand. So as we confess our dependence upon you and our reliance on you, increase our faith to do your work on Earth. In Jesus's name, we pray. Amen.*

Prayer for the Body of Christ

Father, as your children, we have been called according to your Word and the drawing of your Holy Spirit, and we answered the call to leave this world of darkness and walk into and according to your most marvelous light. As born-again believers, help us in our daily walk to remain steadfast and immovable and always abounding in the work of the Lord, for it will not be in vain.

Help us never to shrink back and to stand on your word, and after we've done all that we can, we just stand. Help us to learn that surrender and obedience do not mean we are weak, but it means we are putting our trust in you and we are being made strong in you for we no longer rely on self but casting all our care upon you because you care for us. Help us to understand when we rely on ourselves, we leave ourselves open to doubt and disappointment, but when we place all things in your hands, seek your face, and give you control, we can give thanks for what is to come because we know you have a great track record and doeth all things well.

Teach us, Lord, to apply wisdom to our days and apply the Word mixed with faith to our lives daily. Help us not to live materialistically but to be like Solomon and ask God for wisdom for He provides all the riches we could ever want or need, for He owns a cattle on a thousand hills. He has never seen the righteous forsaken nor his seed begging bread. Show us, Lord, how to be our brother's keeper and to encourage one another and spur one another to godliness.

Show us that when we come together, it should be a time of refreshing, that we come to mutually encourage one another and have a time of fellowship. Teach us early in our walk the way of *repentance and to have a forgiving nature, for when we forgive, the Father forgives our trespasses. Show us how to love our brethren and those who are in authority over us that are watchmen over our souls, and to always intercede one for another.*

Let us be a people who will uphold the man of God whom God has placed over us and to come into agreement for his vision like those in the day of Moses when the vision aligns with God's Word and his will, and let us be the people God has called us to be. In Jesus's name. Amen.

Names of the Trinity

N	E	L	S	H	A	D	D	A	I	W
I	I	I	O	R	L	E	J	L	O	P
A	Z	S	N	T	P	E	U	R	T	R
N	K	T	S	O	H	L	D	O	S	I
O	I	M	H	I	A	O	G	A	I	N
D	N	E	I	R	F	H	E	P	D	C
A	G	V	P	G	O	I	O	A	K	E
R	O	C	O	R	T	M	P	H	E	O
S	F	D	L	E	H	S	E	P	N	F
Y	K	E	R	O	G	R	I	A	U	P
A	I	L	E	O	I	Y	E	R	A	E
D	N	I	M	J	L	E	R	U	H	A
F	G	V	E	E	R	H	E	M	Q	C
O	S	E	E	H	O	L	Y	O	N	E
T	O	R	D	O	C	D	W	L	Y	S
N	N	E	E	V	K	O	A	A	A	N
E	L	R	R	A	N	G	L	H	W	O
I	A	M	B	H	A	I	S	S	E	M
C	R	E	A	T	O	R	S	V	O	E
N	R	E	H	T	A	F	A	S	F	G
A	B	B	A	H	T	U	R	T	I	A

(*) 3-words in 1

Abba	Elohim	King of Kings	Redeemer
Adonai	Father	Lawyer	Rock
Alpha	Friend	Light	Shalom
Ancient of Days	God	Lord-Of-Host (*)	Son
Christ	Holy One	Messiah	Son ship
Creator	I am	Nissi	Truth
Deliverer	Jehovah	Omega	Tsidkenu
El Roi	Jireh	Prince of Peace	Way
El Shaddai	Judge	Rapha	Word of God

Prayer of Thanksgiving

Give thanks with a grateful heart. When we look over our lives and where God has brought us from and brought us through, we could only stop and say, "Thank you, Lord." We often wonder what took us so long to surrender our lives. We have much to be thankful for each and every day, from the ability to open our eyes at the beginning of the day, to all the things we take for granted, like having the full movement of our limbs. Recognizing that all of these many blessings come of thee, O Lord, and are blessings of God that we need to give thanks for. Lord, let us be thankful in the small things of life as well as the large. Although we are not thankful for our trials, they too serve a purpose and are part of the plans God has for our lives.

The he book of James 1:2-4 (Amp) says, 2 Consider it wholly joyful, my brethren, whenever you are enveloped in or encounter trials of any sort or fall into various temptations.

3 Be assured and understand that the trial and proving of your faith bring out endurance and steadfastness and patience.

4 Let endurance, steadfastness, and patience have full play and do a thorough work, so that you may be (people) perfectly and fully developed (with no defects), lacking in nothing.

Remember the Word says we will have trials but they only help to shape and mold us, for without tests there is no testimony. So give thanks in all things for they help to mold us and mature us for kingdom work and kingdom building; so give thanks and glorify your Father in heaven. In Jesus's name. Amen.

Some Books in the Bible

D	E	U	T	E	T	O	N	O	M	Y	A	S
A	C	C	S	J	O	N	A	H	S	H	G	N
N	O	C	N	A	N	S	U	D	O	X	E	A
I	L	S	A	M	U	E	L	S	N	Y	N	I
E	O	E	I	E	W	B	E	R	G	H	E	H
L	S	G	S	S	E	A	D	S	O	T	S	T
A	S	D	E	L	H	R	U	I	F	O	I	N
M	I	U	H	N	T	O	J	H	S	M	S	I
E	A	J	P	O	T	M	O	C	I	A	R	
N	N	O	E	L	A	A	S	A	L	T	M	O
T	S	G	N	R	M	N	H	L	O	H	L	C
A	W	A	H	H	E	S	U	A	M	E	E	A
T	E	L	A	C	O	M	A	M	O	S	V	S
I	R	A	I	L	S	J	I	J	N	S	I	N
O	B	T	N	E	Z	R	A	A	T	A	T	A
N	E	I	A	I	K	E	H	C	H	L	I	I
S	H	A	H	K	U	K	A	H	S	O	C	P
N	K	N	P	E	H	U	I	T	U	N	U	P
A	R	S	E	Z	A	L	D	U	T	I	S	I
H	A	R	Z	E	C	H	A	R	I	A	H	L
U	M	S	G	N	I	K	B	C	T	N	A	I
M	P	S	A	L	M	J	O	B	A	S	B	H
P	E	T	E	R	N	O	M	E	L	I	H	P

Acts	Hebrews	Lamentations	Psalm
Amos	Hosea	Leviticus	Romans
Colossians	James	Luke	Ruth
Corinthians	Jeremiah	Malachi	Samuel
			Song of
Daniel	Job	Mark	Solomon
Deuteronomy	Joel	Matthew	Thessalonians
Ephesians	John	Micah	Timothy
Exodus	Jonah	Nahum	Titus
Ezekiel	Joshua	Obadiah	Zechariah
Ezra	Jude	Peter	Zephaniah
Galatians	Judges	Philemon	
Genesis	Kings	Philippians	

Prayer of Refreshing

Dear God, Our Father, we give you thanks and praise for another opportunity to be able to commune with you in the freshness of a brand new day. We beseech thee, O Lord, for a fresh in-filling of your Holy Spirit. Early in the morning, our souls shall rise to thee and as we rise, we give thanks for another day and another opportunity for refreshing, filling, and reviving of our spirit, our bodies, our minds, and our souls. Before the enemy thinks he is allowed a foothold into the very essence of our being and our day, Lord, we say refresh and revive us once again.

We surrender all that we are and our will unto you, dear Lord, to be filled with your Spirit and be refreshed, revived, and renewed. We leave nothing to chance because we know a God that does not operate in chance but knows the beginning from the end, he knows every hair that is on our head and has a purpose and a plan for your life and mine.

Seek the face of the Father and find refreshment for your soul. If you are thirsty, come and drink from the fountain that never runs dry and replenish your soul. If you are hungry, come, feast on the Word of God, which is manna from heaven that will not only sustain you but bring you through the rough patches of life when you could not see your way through, like the children of Israel going on their journey, away from the clutches of the Egyptians.

Ask God to refresh you and he will restore your soul. He said, "Ask and it shall be added unto to you, Seek and ye shall find, Knock and the door shall be opened." Come aside and be refreshed by his Word, in fellowship and in service unto the King of Kings and the Lord of Lords and you will never again be the same.
In Jesus's name, we pray. Amen.

My Prayer of Being in God's Presence

Lord, how sweet it is to be in your presence. To enjoy the time spent in the quietness of the moments of fellowship and the refreshing of my soul, and for providing a secret place where I can read and meditate in and on Your Word and "pray to thy Father which is in secret; and thy Father which seeth in secret shall reward thee openly" as written in Matthew 6:6 (KJV) Also "He that dwelleth in the secret place of the most High shall abide under the shadow of the Almighty" as written in Psalm 91:1(KJV). Thank you for the time of refreshing and bringing to mind family and friends and to have the opportunity to intercede on their behalf. I pray that they may be strengthened and made whole in their body, mind, and soul and be filled and open their hearts to receive your salvation. But first, Father, I ask that you forgive me for any sinful wrongdoing knowingly or unknowingly committed, that was unpleasing to you, so that you may hear my heart's cry, and cleanse me from all unrighteousness and lead me in a plain path.

Show me how to be my brother's keeper, "For I am not ashamed of the gospel of Christ: for it is the power of God unto salvation to every one that believeth; to the Jew first, and also to the Greek" as told to us in Romans 1:16 (KJV). Your word also says in Psalm 16:11 (AMP), "You will show me the path of life; in Your presence is fullness of joy, at Your right hand there are pleasures forevermore." My prayer is that we also experience this and give thanks. Thank you for the times of praising you in song and in dance, in tongues and in weeping. Thank you for downloading songs into my spirit that magnify and glorify you, and that will one day encourage someone and make them think about you and see what I see about you and realize who you are to me, a mighty God, my Rock and my Salvation, my hope and help, my sustainer and keeper. Thank you for the times of fellowship with the saints in praise and worship and adoration to you, O Lord Most High.

Truly it is awesome and uplifting to be in your presence, and for this I am glad to be called a child of God. I pray that everyone who reads this and calls on the Name of Jesus can experience what I experience every day and live in your presence. May I serve you with my whole heart and understand that I have been saved to serve as you have shown us the way by your example. May we follow you, search your word, and ask for understanding and walk in the way everlasting as you are the way the truth and the life. Help us to be still and know that you are God, and as we trust in and rely upon you and release our will to you, we can walk victorious because of you. Fill us with Your Spirit and may your Spirit guide us into all truth. In Jesus's precious name, we pray with thanksgiving. Amen.

May we mutually encourage one another by our faith and stay in God's presence.

Part Three

"Family Circle"

A Prayer and Blessing for My Daughter Kelly

Father, bless my child this precious gift
You gave her to me it was not hit or miss
You gave her a beautiful voice to sing
Your praises and let your anthem ring

You gave her a creative spirit to bless others with
All these things you gave her are your gifts
As she celebrates her special day
Bless her with health and strength to enjoy and play
Let her know I love her always no matter what we say and do
And she will always be precious to me and you

The Blessing:
You are my gift from God and you are truly blessed
You bring joy most times so we won't dwell on the rest
As girls we fight a bit, but I will always love you
And enjoy your creative spirit and the loving things you do

Remember as you get older I will be there for you more but you will feel like you need me less and less
So let's enjoy the time we have and make it the very best
You have helped me to bend when it comes to our little pet
And it warms my heart that you are happy and our animal's needs are met

Continue to keep God at the center of all you say and do
And family and friends will respect you,, and God the Father will be
most pleased too.
My prayer is that you be in good health and enjoy every moment of
life on your birthday
It is a gift from God for a special little lady, may He bless you each
and every day.

I love you always,
Mommy

Child-Rearing Challenges

I sat back upon my bed one day
Shaking my head in total dismay
At the decision I made a long, long time ago
To rear this child of mine, boy, did I not know

The challenges, the pain, the patience it would take
The sacrifices in my life I would have to make
You thought the changing of pampers and sleepless nights were hard
That was in the beginning, a mere attempt of the start

One day she was all meek and oh, so mild
A beautiful baby you adored, fussed over, and bragged, "That's my child"
And then the day came when she had her own voice and could answer you back
No more silence and adoring looks from you, you were being dealt a new deck

Before you know it, here comes the next stage of her life
Nursery, building her own character, individuality, and spice
But watch out I say the challenge is drawing nigh
As you chuckled with an anticipating sigh

The moods, mouth, and the changes of the character you did not expect
Are the rearing challenges looking rosy yet?
Are you having fun with the major changes in your life?
Rearing this child through the heartaches and strife

Now school is upon you, and so too is the mouth and the attitudes
And the clothing, the peer pressure, adolescence from which it all
alludes
Oh, help me please, did I really mean to go down this road
Too late, you can handle it; God has prepared you for this load

He will equip you if you trust him with your challenge and charge
Because for Him it's a small task although for you it is large.
So enjoy the child rearing years, rule with the Word of God
And although she may stray, she will remember from whence she
trod
For a foundation laid right is according to God's Word
It's the best you can offer, live it out so it is seen and heard.

Father, Equip Me for Life

Looking back over my life I used to think I had it made
A good job, friends to boot, even money I had saved
I didn't drink much, didn't smoke, lived a pretty decent life
Lived a calm and peaceful existence without enmity or strife

Picked up a few accolades that made my parents proud
Wasn't boastful most of the time and my demeanor wasn't loud
Pretty much kept to myself and though I had it made
But something was missing in my life although the best plans of life
were made

I have a loving child, a good job, and a house I call my home
And sometimes it's hard to keep a perspective that this is all here on
loan
For although I allow God to equip me for life, this is not my final
resting place
I must learn to seek him first, trust and rely on him as I run this race

So Father, equip me for life to raise my beautiful child
Help me to teach her to be more like you in character and style
Show me how to live as a single mother, show me your plan for my life
Let me know your purpose and plan and make it clear and concise

Teach me how to listen and guide me along the way
So that what I do in my household will bring joy, peace, and praise to
your name each day.

Father, Be Reconciled with Your Offspring

A father is supposed to be the head of his household
He is to set the example for his spouse and children and should stand
bold
So Father, tell me are you here today or gone astray
Be reconciled to your offspring to show him the way

Father, are you showing love for your helpmate or just spreading
your seed
You were not put on this earth just to fool around and breed
God set the example for all of mankind to follow
To be upright not just in stature but to leave a good legacy for
tomorrow

Father, are you estranged from your offspring or are you there
Are you showing them a positive role model for them to adhere
Or are you relying on the mother to take up your role
And leaving her the legacy that will be foretold

Father, your offspring are depending on you
Looking for your guidance and wisdom too
You have the ability to help them avoid enmity and strife
Even if you are not in the home, make sure you are involved in their
life.

So Father, be reconciled with your offspring!
It will be the best legacy and imprint you can leave.

Memories of My Grandfather
"Gone but never forgotten"

Papa,
As I behold your figure before me
No longer to see this earthly body again
I reflect on the memories as shadows
Like the dawn of a day at an end

I remember the times we shared
With laughter and sometimes with tears
And sitting and praying together
To dispel your earthly fears
I gather them up as sweet memories
To hold dear for the coming years

Now rest, my sweet, in the Lord's hands
For there will be no more pain to endure
As you made your peace in this world
And made your calling and election sure

I miss our joyful times of singing
But now you sing with the angels
Remember, bonds can never be broken
When they are knit together with the perfect cord of love
I love you, and I miss you
Rest peacefully in the Comforter's Arms

Happy 40ᵗʰ Anniversary, Mom and Dad
"You've reached a Milestone"

What does it mean when you have been married for forty years?

It means that you have raised your children and in some cases your grandchildren too
It means you've seen changes in life on many levels that have affected you
It means that you've learned the lessons called flexibility and compromise
It means that you have endured much and are truly wise

It means that love has and is still covering a multitude of things
In order that you can say I'm still hanging in there despite life's swings
It means that you learned to agree to disagree even when you don't want to
And bite your tongue to keep the peace, and do what you have to do

It means struggling to make ends meet when you didn't have a dime
And wondering sometimes where your next meal is coming from at some point in time
It means being proud of your children because of the morals that you set
And knowing that when you raised them you did your very best

It means that you still look at one another and know there is still love
For better or for worse as you pledged to the Lord above
The day you said those vows and took them seriously
Has brought us to forty years later to celebrate your feat

With Much Love I Salute and Celebrate with you today.
God Bless you both is my prayer each and every day.

Mother, Who Are You?

As I gaze in the mirror at this tired silhouette at the end of the workday
As I leave one job and begin another, picking up the children from school
As I sit with my daughter to read her book and do her homework too
As I begin to cook dinner and set the table for the evening meal
I ask, who are you, "I'm a 'Working' mother," she replied

As I care for my ill child, clean the house, and fight to keep my strength
As I darn the clothing and make an outfit out of a scrap of fabric
As I bow my knee to pray to keep you safe and my household too
I ask, who are you, "I'm a 'Caring' mother," she replied

As I sit with a hospitalized loved one reading and speaking the Word of God over him
As I extend my hand to show love to some little one whom I never met before
As I love unconditionally this life I brought into this world
I ask, who are you, "I'm a 'Compassionate' mother," she replied

As my heart breaks for a troubled child
As I care for foster children with troubled parents
As I play the roll of a big sister in someone's life
I ask, who are you, "I'm a 'Sensitive' mother," she replied

As I cry out to God against our youth, attacking each other out of peer pressure
As I storm heaven's doors to voice my concern against drunk driving

As I take a stand to educate the next generation with truth and righteousness
I ask, who are you, "I'm a 'God-fearing' mother," she replied

Mother, your work is never done. For you were called to be:
Home to the homeless
Help to the helpless
Mother to the motherless
Prayer warriors for the hopeless
And whatever odd job falls in between
Thank God for you, for the strength He gave you to endure
And that special something within that lets us know who we are
"We are Mothers."

Dad, What Hat Are You Wearing Today

The Family Dad:
Hello, Dad, it's me
Remember when I used to sit upon your knee
You would tell me a story of the days of old
I listened so intently to the story being told
Dad, you are wearing your hat that says put family first

The Father Gone Astray:
I look around I do not see
Any Dad in front of me
All I see is Mom, relatives,, and others in my life
This is the absentee father, leaving void and strife
Father, this is not the example you want to set for your loved one
Be there for your offspring; don't be replaced by anything or anyone
Dad, this is not the hat you want to wear, for it only leads to heartbreak and despair

The Wise Man:
Hey, Dad, I'm having problems in school with my friends
The peer pressure and the studies have me at my wits' end
I'm there for you my child, here's some good advice
We will seek God's Word for an answer; your burdens will be made light
Sometimes I don't have all the answers but I know someone who does
He's the Lord, my counselor and friend, and he lives above
Okay, Dad, now you are wearing your hat that says I'm using wisdom

The Father walking with God:
Dad, you have taken your rightful place
You are walking with God not by sight but by faith
You are setting the example for your house and home
Remembering that you are not walking this road alone
If this is you, Dad, I know what hat you are wearing
It's your hat of salvation, for God you are yearning

Dad, pick the right hat and wear it proud
Be the best Dad you can be, instead of running with the crowd
Your offspring will benefit by the best choice you make
Remember you have the power to leave a good legacy or destruction
in your wake

Happy Father's Day to all the Dads and please choose your hat
wisely. May God richly bless you today and always!

Mother's Day Greetings for My Family

God Bless You, Mother
All the Days of Your Life
A Daughter's Prayer

Mother, God has blessed me with you
And He entrusted you with the tools to mold me and he knew you
would know what to do
You have taught me how to love unconditionally
And how to save for a rainy day to secure myself financially
You've demonstrated that sometimes love means putting others
before yourself
And that family is more important than a job or wealth
I am glad to have you as an example and a model worthy to repeat
It is truly a blessing and a testament to strive for and one day meet
Blessings to you, my Mother, today and all of your days
May the face of God continue to shine upon you, for one day you
will give Him praise.
Happy Mother's Day, Mom
With love from your youngest daughter

A Mother's Day Wish
For My Sister
Sis, we share something in common
That makes us who we are today, Mothers of Daughters (Yeah)
They have brought us smiles and tears
And sometimes we'd like to trade them in, but instead we've loved
them through the years

You've played your part and they are all grown up
Although caring for them will never stop
So my wish is that you concentrate on you today
Pamper yourself, relax a little, laugh a lot, and play
And may you be blessed in all that you do
For the Lord will watch over and take care of you.
Happy Mother's Day, Marchelle
With much love
From your baby sister

A Sister in a Sister
What a Blessed Celebration for Mother's Day

Sometimes we take for granted who we really are
We are mothers, we're sisters, but really we are much more by far
As mothers we are called to mold the life entrusted to our hand
But as sisters of the Most High God, there is an even bigger plan
I'm blessed we have much more in common than our looks our children and our genes
We are called to be mothers in Christ, setting the example and planting seed
So as we share in the vineyard, let's plant them in our family today
And make this Mother's Day one we will never forget as we bow our knees to pray

Happy Mother's Day, Maxine
With much love and God's continual favor
From your baby sister

Beauty in the Eyes of a child

Innocent, trusting are the eyes of a child
Clinging to your every word in the twinkle of their smile
Vulnerable and open, taking it all in like a sponge
Is the beauty in the eye of a child, and to you she will lunge?

No fear they show, for each step is new
For they have not lived and learned, some things can harm you
There are no inhibitions to hold them back
Life for them is an adventure and discoveries they have not yet tapped

They climb high mountains, and drop from swings far and wide
Like the rollercoasters of life, it's a thrill they feel inside
That's the beauty in the eyes of a child, right now, nothing to fear
Trusting, oblivious of adversity and harm without a care

The Word of God says for us to come to Christ just like one of them
For they only know the simplicity of things and parents are their guiding hands
So if we have childlike faith and abandon ourselves and all we know
Salvation is the reward we gain and eternity and heaven is where we'll go

So live life, love always, laugh, and let go
And experience the beauty in the eyes of a child.

How Young People Communicate

Skype is where it is at today
Facebook, Twitter are here to stay
They see their friends and talk all day long
You would not know it, for in the evening the communication continues on.

Playing games outside like we did as kids
Seems to be a thing of the past, Oh no, that's what you did!
Every now and then they find something they think is cool
Like climbing a pile of rubble, rolling down it, and playing the fool

Oh dear, guess what! This is really fun
I gave my electronics a break and enjoyed some one on one
With a friend around, hey, it's cool
I don't have to always be on a chat to have fun, guess what, "Games rule"

But hanging with my buds, truly is all that
Swapping chats, listening to tunes, man that's Fat

Is this how the young folks talk
As long as it keeps clean, I'm cool with the walk
So go ahead, young folks, communicate
Enjoy your friendships, before it's too late.

Prayer for Mom

Father, I thank you for allowing my mom to see seventy-five years of life. May something that is said, done, sung, or heard touch her heart. May she draw close to you and feel your presence. Father, I pray that you give her all the desires of her heart and bless her with continual health and strength to see many more years.

I pray that you bless her in her finances. I pray you bless her in her rising and her lying down, in her labor and in her leisure. I pray that the joy of the Lord will be her strength and her portion. I pray, Father, that she be free of pain and walk in health, and that there will be peace in her household, peace in her heart, and peace in her mind.

I pray that she will continue to be a blessing to her family, friends, community, and that her children will continue to call her blessed. Father, I thank you for this role model you have given to us on loan to show strength, love, and compassion with a sense of family value and togetherness. May you continue to bless and keep her for all the days of her life. In Jesus's name, I pray. Amen.

Bask in one of your favorite songs as your prayer:
Hear my cry, O Lord, attend unto my prayer
From the ends of the earth will I cry unto thee
When my heart is overwhelmed, lead me to the rock
That is higher than I, that is higher than I.
Mom, you can cry out, for the Father wants to answer you.

What Does the Word Mother Mean to Me?

M – Mother, Matriarch, Minister, Motivational Speaker, Memory Bank, Manner
O – Outstanding, Open, Over-protective, Overjoyed, and Outspoken
T – Tender, Tangible, Tested, Tried, True, Testimony, and Tenacious
H – Helpful, Historian, Heaven-sent, Humble, Host, and Hilarious
E – Exceptional, Excited, Enthusiastic, Empathetic, and Emotional
R – Reliable, Responsible, Resilient, and Respectful.

As I look over the world, many mothers fit the characteristics listed above
There are so many more to list, but the most important not listed is LOVE
"Mother" has so many meanings for so many people, that words cannot say,
They don't fit into the acronym above of the lettering displayed

Mother has been a solid rock on which I can stand
She has always been there when I need her to lend a helping hand
She is there to share the good news and to hear my troubles too
And encourages me during the rough patches when I don't know what to do

Mother is the one who holds the family together through the sunshine and the rain
She's also the one to correct you when you are doing wrong even though it costs her pain
She loves you unconditionally even when your actions are not pleasing to her

*She stands firm on discipline and correction so your foolishness
doesn't continue to occur*

*A mother feels the pain of loss for her loved one more than anyone
else
As she bore the first pains of her child at birth deep inside herself
She prays that her children will exhibit the good values that she has
taught
And be a model example she can be proud of in word, deed, and thought
A mother is love, peace, kindness, and a place to run to for shelter
That's what a Mother means to me and that's what truly matters.*

Yesterday's Friendship, Today's Wedding Bliss

Many people are together for a lifetime
And never make it to more than friendships that grow over time
Some have children to carry on their name
With unspoken commitments and lingering hopes, but it's not the same

Our lives together have brought us struggles and sometimes pain
But we weathered the storms, through the sunshine and the rain
We've seen many friends marry and separate from each other
But we have stood the test of time and stayed together
We've seen many people fall, in and out of love
But our love has made us stronger, it must be from above

We have grown together and now you are mine
We have created a bond that has stood the test of time
Today we pledge to take all those experiences with us, we have fought and overcome
Today I marry my friend and two shall become one

There have been many yesterdays that we've had together
We shared good times and many years of laughter
We probably even talked a time or two of making it more than this
And look where we've come, today this is Wedding bliss

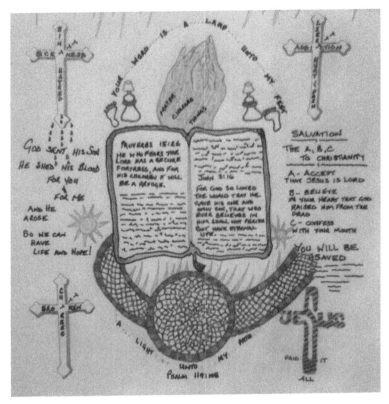

Author's drawing

Part Four

"Lord, Speak to Me"

God Is a God of Order

As I have read the account of the instruction given to Moses back in the day
Not only do I believe it, but know it, that God is a God of order, I can truly say
He is precise, detailed, and meticulous in every way
Leaving nothing to chance, he made sure everything was put in its place

Just like the word he gave to Moses long ago
He is also meticulous with us if we let God and tell self to just "let go"
He will give us instructions to lead us and guide us if we give Him our will
All we need to say is "Order my steps, Lord, show me your way and let me be still."

Of course this is easier said than done
Because this old flesh of ours thinks this is a war it should have won
But fear not, let the God of order direct your way today
For truly it will bring blessings, joy, and peace your way

Not only will your obstacles seem insignificant compared to most men
But the God of order will see you out of each trial and allow you to stand.

For we are more than conquerors through Him that saved us and gave Himself for us!

Am I a Source of Encouragement?

When we see a new convert in the faith, what do we do or say
As seasoned Christians, do we shy away or offer to encourage them along the way
The Word talks about the parable of the "Sower", what part do we play
Are we helping our brethren to grow or are we letting them drift away

We know by way of God's Word that there are seeds that the enemy will pluck as soon as it falls
But we have the ability to change that scenario in some cases by helping the new convert to stand tall
Partner with people who have given God their heart, mind, and soul
By sharing the truth of the gospel with them, it should never grow old

Be a source of encouragement and guide that fallen seed toward good soil
And help your fellow sister or brother up from under life's temptations and toils
For there are three types of seeds sown as referenced similarities in the parable of the Sower in (Matthew 13:1-23 - KJV) today
And we never know which one will be someone's fate

So share God's Word, plant a seed, nurture it and water it today
To reap a harvest for Christ that in heaven your crown will repay
Be a source of encouragement whenever you can
For you may avoid someone's seed from falling on barren land

We're praying for much more seeds to fall on good soil in our land
So we can rejoice with the angels, for the harvest is ripe and at hand
Be a blessing and share God's Holy Word
As it is the greatest gift I have ever heard.

Be encouraged and an encouragement. In Jesus's name. Amen.

Believing—Is It Only What I Can See?

"What makes us believe?"
Is it what we can see?
Is it tangible?
Is it possible?
Is it plausible?
Is it a gut feeling?
Or is it unseen and faith?
What is it for you?

The Word of God says in Hebrews 11:1 (KJV),
Faith is the substance of things hoped for, the evidence of things not
yet seen.
It also talks of Speaking those things that are not as though they were.

Is belief based on your hopes and dreams, like I hope to get a bike
when I am sixteen, or that one day you hope to have a house!

Is your belief something that has a foundation that is outside of your
hands and control?
Or is it solely dependent upon you?

Belief and faith go hand in hand
As you place your hope and trust in God he will help you to
understand
We learn as believers to trust the unseen God whom we cannot trace
his hand
For we know there is someone bigger than you and I, this is the
evidence of our faith

The Word also tells us to speak those things that are not as though they were
For what seems impossible with the natural eye is the norm in God's sphere

Edna Tatum, the songwriter of "Come Ye Disconsolate" penned in a song one day, talking about the substance of faith. "You can't see around that curve but you've got enough substance right now to know that God is up ahead working things out."
We cannot see the wind but we believe that we feel it on our skin. We don't even see the air but we breathe it into our lungs by faith and we live.

We have not seen God the Father or Jesus Christ his Son, but yet we believe because we have accepted Him and his Spirit speaks. We see people recovering from illnesses when the doctor says all else has failed but we believe by faith and see the manifestation of God's miraculous work.

In John 20:29 (KJV) Jesus saith unto him, "Thomas, because thou hast seen me, thou hast believed: blessed are they that have not seen, and yet have believed." Next time when you have experienced something wonderful that you can't touch or did not see beforehand and cannot explain, I dare you to just believe.
And remember it does not need to be seen, felt, or you deem it possible, just believe.

You ask is it tangible, some things are and some things are far beyond our reach
But when we put our trust in the Father, it becomes what we ask in faith and seek
He told us to ask in his name with the right motive in mind
And watch the manifestation of our blessing brought forth in time

Have you experienced something tangible that you did not believe? Like the woman with the issue of blood, as many pressed their way and pressed up against Jesus, we must press with purpose, faith, and belief for healing. The woman was made whole, and Jesus felt virtue go out of him to heal her.

Is it plausible you say, Oh yes, it surely is
With God all things are possible and plausible to receive and give
This faith walk is something special, and prayer, submission, and obedience is the key
Faith unlocks the door to blessings; God is the answer for you and me

In Matthew 8:6-8 (NIV-The Thompson's Chain Reference Bible), This was the account of the centurion and Jesus, "6. Lord, he said, my servant lies at home paralyzed and in terrible suffering. 7. Jesus said to him, I will go and heal him. 8. The centurion replied, Lord, I do not deserve to have you come under my roof. But just say the word, and my servant will be healed". (Amp) His faith let him know that it was plausible and reassured him that he did not have to see God's hand touch the man but he just needed to speak a word and he would be healed. For we walk by faith and not by sight. Many of the unseen things we will leave in God's hands and just simply believe with childlike faith and trust.

Remember don't trust your gut, it has failed you many times
Jesus is the way the truth and the life, come on, make up your mind
So I implore you now, seek out the God I serve and trust
And believing will no longer be just what you can see, or what you feel in your gut
It will be a life-changing experience, and an everlasting hope
The synopsis above is not just an invitation or a tactfully written note
This is an invitation of salvation! So tell me, "Is believing only what you can see?"

Lord, What Must I Sacrifice?

Many people don't know what it is to sacrifice
What is sacrifice?
Sacrifice is something you give up to obtain something you want or
that is far better than what you have.

Lord, show me what I need to sacrifice
To bring me closer to you and be more pleasing in your sight
Help me to let go of the grip of things that hold me down
Let me not have you pry them from me, but learn to release them
and not be bound

Let me see that you will supply my every need
Reassure me that you have watered everything I sowed to seed
As you have poured out blessing toward me I can truly say
My life has changed for the better, since you came my way

It is said in your word (1 Samuel 15:22b, AMP) that to obey is better
than sacrifice
So help us to learn this lesson early to be at peace and not in strife
And as we go along life's journey and meander through life's way
We can be glad your spirit drew us and we invited you in to stay.

Thank you for being my Savior and Lord.

May the Work I've Done Speak for Me

Lord this is a simple prayer, uttered from my heart
I pray, dear Lord, that I have shared your word in whole or at least in part
To make a change in someone's life and show a reflection of you
In how I conduct myself, in the words I speak, and in what I do

May this journey that I take each day be an opportunity to share
Your goodness, your mercy, that you love mankind and care
And that you hold your arms outstretched waiting to take them in
As you choose them, we pray they accept you and turn away from sin

Teach us, Lord, to live each day as a reflection of you
Dying daily to this old flesh and by your spirit be renewed
For in this flesh there is no good, unless we take on your righteousness
Repenting for sins known and unknown, these I must confess

Let my voice be an instrument to draw man unto thee
Let them hear your word via songs I sing, see you and not me
As I pray with my child or friend or a foe
May the words that I speak, bring life and go forth to show

That Lord you are on the throne and all glory belongs to you
I am just a vessel, obedient to carry your message through
So Lord may the work I've done truly speak for me
May it liberate and go forth and set many a captive free.

Morning Blessing

"Words of encouragement to a new convert"

As God has given us life another day
We can only praise Him for He has made a way

He opened up the window and showed us his beauty once more
And poured out a new blessing on us He kept safely in store

He said, "Come, my children, these riches I have stored up for you
Just follow my Word and precepts and I will see you through"

So continue to praise Him and to walk in His way
He will guide and protect you, come what may.

Give him thanks, for this new day you have never seen before
And greet the Father, Son, and Holy Spirit, whom you'll learn to
love and adore

What I Am Thankful For

I am thankful for another day that I am able to see
And for the many blessings that God has given me
I am thankful for the roof that has been placed over my head
And for each night when I lie down in my very comfortable bed

I am thankful for my teachers who help to mold my mind
And for every day that I can share, hope and to be kind
I am thankful for parents who take care of my needs and wants too
When I look over my short life I'm thankful for things both old and new

I guess if you really stop and look at what's in front of you
There are many things to be truly thankful for, this is really true
So if we are always up in arms about things being so hard and unfair
Let's look at what we should be thankful for and look to the ones who
really care

If you are shown love by a parent, church, teacher, or a friend
Be thankful instead of ungrateful and ask what fence can I mend?
Each one of us has a responsibility of what we do with our life
So each day that God wakes you up be thankful for his grace and supply

It's precious; don't let anyone or anything sway you the wrong way,
be positive and make someone else thankful to have crossed your path
For your impression can have a rippling effect of good that will truly last
These are just a few things that I am thankful for and thank God that
I am
For being his child; his voice onn the Earth and knowing He is my friend

A thankful heart is like good medicine, it brings forth good results
So be thankful!

When I Place It in God's Hands

We never know what a day may bring
We never know if we will have a song to sing
We never know what toils of life will bring
But it will all be better when we place it in God's hands

We do not know if we will see tomorrow
We never know if we will live joyously or have sorrow
We never know if we will be a lender or have to borrow
But God has a plan when we place it in his hands

What we see with our natural eye is not always what is there
What we encounter each day of our lives is not always fair
When we open our hearts to others not everyone will care
But it makes a difference when we place it first in God's hand

Though life may not always deal us the hand we expect
Or our families or colleagues show us our due respect
But there is a crown waiting for his children lest we forget
When we place our lives in God's hand

Now remember this is not my words, but his alone
When we ask God in our hearts to make us his home
He will lead us and guide us and help us to stand
When we place it all in God's hands

Why Suffer Wrath over Obedience

As I read God's word I see so clearly what it says to his people
But as many times it's told to us the flesh and stubbornness hold fast
like a steeple
Let go, I say to our foolish wishes and desires
Give up your selfish whims of pride; stop getting burned in the fires
He shows us how to live, in obedience by his will and his way
Sometimes it's hard to surrender to God and we insist on going astray
How many plagues must we endure and how many deaths must we
see before we pay attention
How many lives must we cry over and guilt must we carry before
our redemption
Narrow is the path many will not take, we know this for the Word
has already been told
But don't despair and don't give up for there is more work to be done
and more Gospel to be shared for a harvest of souls

David was a man after God's heart but he did not always please the
Lord
Many times he wanted to do things his way and live by the sword
But God showed him favor many times because David knew God
was his source
And he knew in order to get back on track, prayer, supplication, and
surrender was his course
I'm speaking to myself as I write these words because many times I stray
But trust and know that I cannot make it on my own and I know
that Jesus is the only way
He is my waking moment, my strength, and in Him I put my trust
And to go thru any day without acknowledging who he is to me, is
unheard of "I must"

And although I may be like the prophets of old straying from time to time
I want to be sure it's less straying and more praying and walking in his will not mine
Lord always give me fresh insight through your Word, and teach me to be more like thee
Never puffed up but humble, avoiding war and looking to bring peace

Look for opportunities to share a kind word to someone who has never heard the gospel before
And increase God's kingdom and make a difference in saving a dying world.
You'll never regret it and the angels will rejoice.

Mothers in the Word are Mothers of the Word

There are mothers in the Bible that we can identify with
Some are portrayed as ashamed (Hagar Ishmael's mother)
Some are portrayed as wise (Moses's mother)
Some are portrayed as dedicated (Hannah, Samuel's mother)
Some are portrayed as faithful and strong through adversity (Naomi, Mahlon, and Kilion's mother)
And some are portrayed as pure and blessed (Mary, Jesus's mother)
But the Word of God teaches us that we should "Honor thy father and thy mother: that thy days may be long upon the land which the Lord thy God giveth thee," Exodus 20:12 (KJV)

Hagar, maidservant of Sarah, was made to feel ashamed after following instructions, but God showed her and Ishmael favor.
Mother, have you ever felt ashamed of something you've done, something you have said or how you've lived your life?
Know that if you trust and rely on God, no circumstances of life (with repentance) can prevent you from receiving His forgiveness, love, and favor.

Will you hide your child away in a basket and send him down the river like Moses's mother did that he might live?
A mother's protective nature will lead her to do things that are unheard of, and seemingly out in left field, but with God all things are possible according to His will and your faith.

Samuel's mother, Hannah, was dedicated to the work of the Lord; a prayerful woman who made sure her son was taken care of each time she offered her annual sacrifice.

A mother will take her last dime to make sure her children are cared for; and a praying mother not only sets the example in her household, she also opens the door for God's blessings.

Naomi lost her husband and two sons and thought God had dealt with her bitterly only to have Him bless her through her daughter-in-law.
Some mothers have to endure death and lose all before they receive the ultimate blessings that Jesus has in store for them. And he said to them all, If any man will come after me, let him deny himself (Luke 9:23a, KJV), and forsake those things that are near and dear.

Mary the mother of Jesus—a virgin, obedient and highly favored of God.
Are we mothers of virtue, and what legacy are we leaving our children? Have we learned to surrender to God and walk in obedience to his calling?
As his children through his Spirit enveloping us, we live in his favor daily.
So today, be a mother that gets into the Word, so you can be a mother that lives by the Word.
Command your soul to live, speak, think, and walk God's Word.

A mother demonstrates compassion, and a mother expresses love
A mother is protective, and her intuitions know no bounds
A mother is stern, but her actions show she is fair
A mother is caring but not afraid to share
A mother takes risks when things look hopeless
A mother knows shame, but in God finds forgiveness
A mother knows poverty, but relies on the one true source
A mother knows hatred, but in God finds real love.

Acknowledgments

I would like to take this opportunity to thank individuals who have helped make this book a reality.

To my proof readers, Eloise Tuzo, Marchelle Gibbons, Maxine Harvey, Malodie Julio and Rawle Frederick, your assistance has been invaluable and I am most grateful and delighted to have you onboard.

To my family who have always believed in me and encouraged me in whatever I have set my mind to do.

To my church family who have encouraged me and prayed in agreement with me for this vision.

I acknowledge and give thanks to the Father, Son, and Holy Spirit who is my guide, and my source, for without the Trinity none of this would be possible.

About the Author

Marionette Simmons, a Bermudian native and author of Life's Challenges, Experiences and Blessings *has now ventured farther into the deep and has been blessed to share with you her second book which you now hold in your hand*—God's Promises for the Family Circle. *It seems that this average girl with ordinary dreams has learned that with God, the ordinary becomes extraordinary when you place everything in his hands. It only goes to show that there is nothing average about God's people. She continues to enjoy writing and to have opportunities to bless someone with her words of wisdom and experience fed to her through the inspiration of the Holy Spirit, God's Word, and her life's lessons. Her aims and endeavors are to put God first, her loving daughter next, and all else just falls into place, which allows her to also work, sing, and embark on her latest venture—the production of her very first full-scale gospel CD hopefully to be released in 2015. She was instrumental in releasing a single in her local island on December 19, 2014 entitled, "Savior was Born on Christmas Day" that will be included on the full-scale CD. It was received with gladness by the hearers of God's Word in song and those who joined with her in support by purchasing a copy for a keepsake.*

Writing is still very much a passion of Marionette. Stand in agreement in prayer for more inspired words from her to encourage someone on their life's journey and to have her as an avenue for you to spend time in the presence of God. She hopes and prays one day for her greatest recognition and reward to come from the Father above, when he can say to her, as written in Matthew 25:21(KJV), "Well done, thou good and faithful servant: thou has been faithful over a few things, I will make thee ruler over many things: enter thou into the joy of the Lord." But until then, she enjoys such other recognitions on earth that she receives yearly, as she composes a new Mother's and Father's Day tribute for many to enjoy.

Marionette has dedicated many years to writing and has been inspired by other people's life's experiences, expressions, travels, and her family. Having been encouraged by the many contemporaries who share her Father and Mother's Day poems each year, Marionette decided to step out of her comfort zone again and publish book number two, and also enter the recording world in her soon-to-be-released CD.

After getting her feet wet initially with Life's Challenges, Experiences and Blessings in 2007—it was her first book and a realization of a lifelong dream—there are no holds barred nor obstacles that will prevent her from pressing on to share with the public, her supporters, friends, and readers looking for some hope.

God's Promises for the Family Circle is another blessing and collection of Marionette's work. Enjoy the journey as much as she enjoyed writing it just for you. She looks at this challenge and blessing as a way to continue to let her light shine, and let people know that life always has something new in store for them.

Printed in the United States
By Bookmasters